T0011671

J. J. Watt

By Jon M. Fishman

AMAZING
ATHLETES

Lerner Publications • Minneapolis

Copyright © 2015 by Lerner Publishing Group, Inc.

All rights reserved. International copyright secured. No part of this book may be reproduced, stored in a retrieval system, or transmitted in any form or by any means—electronic, mechanical, photocopying, recording, or otherwise—without the prior written permission of Lerner Publishing Group, Inc., except for the inclusion of brief quotations in an acknowledged review.

Lerner Publications Company
A division of Lerner Publishing Group, Inc.
241 First Avenue North
Minneapolis, MN 55401 USA

For reading levels and more information, look up this title at www.lernerbooks.com.

Library of Congress Cataloging-in-Publication Data

Fishman, Jon M.
     J. J. Watt / by Jon M. Fishman.
        pages cm. — (Amazing athletes)
     Includes index.
     ISBN 978–1–4677–3676–3 (lib. bdg. : alk. paper)
     ISBN 978–1–4677–4588–8 (EB pdf)
     1. Watt, J. J., 1989– 2. Football players—United States—Biography. I. Title.
  GV939.W362F57 2015
  796.332092—dc23 [B]   2014000367

Manufactured in the United States of America
2 – BP – 3/1/15

TABLE OF CONTENTS

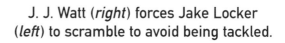

J. J. Watt (*right*) forces Jake Locker (*left*) to scramble to avoid being tackled.

TEXANS STAR

Houston Texans **defensive end** J. J. Watt crouched low to the ground. He bent his knees and used his right arm to support his massive body. Hut, hut! J. J. surged forward. He slammed into the Tennessee Titans player across from him. J. J. used his powerful arms to push the Tennessee player back. Then the Texans star grabbed Tennessee **quarterback** Jake Locker and threw him to the ground. Another **sack** for J. J.!

J. J. (*right*) slams the Tennessee quarterback to the ground.

Houston was taking on Tennessee on September 15, 2013. More than 71,000 fans filled Reliant Stadium in Houston. Cameras flashed and the crowd roared as J. J. sacked the quarterback. The fans expected nothing less from their star.

The Texans had the lead in the second quarter, 7–0. J. J. was confident—with good

Fans cheer for J. J. during the game.

J. J. is known for swatting balls out of the air. He's so good at it that people call him J. J. Swatt.

J. J. runs after the quarterback.

reason. He had been named National Football League (NFL) Defensive Player of the Year in 2012. He'd worked hard to be even better in 2013. "I study myself to see where I can improve my game," J. J. said. "But this **off-season** I also studied other teams to see what their plan might be."

J. J.'s studies paid off again in the third quarter.

J. J. (*lower middle*) tackles Jake Locker again,

He powered his way past a Titans **offensive lineman**. He grabbed Locker and slammed the quarterback to the turf once more. Tennessee was forced to **punt**.

J. J. had Locker and the Titans on the run. But then Tennessee scored two touchdowns in the fourth quarter. The game was tied.

Houston had the ball first in **overtime**. They marched down the field and scored a touchdown. The Texans won the game 30–24!

There were still many games to play in the 2013 season. But J. J. was ready for anything. "I'm like an animal in a cage that you haven't given food to in a while," he said. "As soon as you let me out, something is getting eaten."

J. J. celebrates the Texans' victory.

Waukesha, where J. J. Watt was born, is the seventh-biggest city in Wisconsin.

HOCKEY FAN

John and Connie Watt's first child was born in Waukesha, Wisconsin, on March 22, 1989. They named him Justin James. Everyone called him J. J.

J. J. grew up in nearby Pewaukee with his two younger brothers, Derek and T. J. Hockey is a popular sport in Wisconsin during the long, cold winters. J. J. learned to skate when he was three years old. Since then, hockey has been his favorite sport.

"Hockey, honestly, was my first love," J. J. said in 2013. "I still love it to this day." But hockey costs a lot of money to play. Players need expensive equipment. Teams travel long distances for **tournaments**.

Youth hockey is very popular in J. J.'s home state of Wisconsin.

When he was 13, J. J. stopped competing. "Really, I had to quit," J. J. said. "I have two younger brothers and we were all playing on a travel team, and it was extremely expensive."

Luckily for J. J., he had fun playing other sports as well. He enjoyed baseball, basketball, and track and field. He also loved the thrill of football. The Watt family's backyard was big and open. It was connected to two other similar backyards. Kids from all around the neighborhood would meet in the yards to play football. "It was awesome," J. J. said.

J. J. also played basketball when he was young, like these boys.

Brett Favre was the quarterback for the Green Bay Packers when J. J. was a kid.

J. J. knew that he wanted to play football in high school. But he didn't want to be a defensive end. "I thought the high school quarterback was greater than Brett Favre, greater than any player who ever lived," J. J. said. "I thought he was the coolest man in the entire world."

When J. J. began high school as a first-year student in 2003, he didn't look much like a football player. He was tall and scrawny. But J. J.'s father and uncles are big men. J. J. was still growing. "Everyone would tell us he's going to be a huge kid," said John.

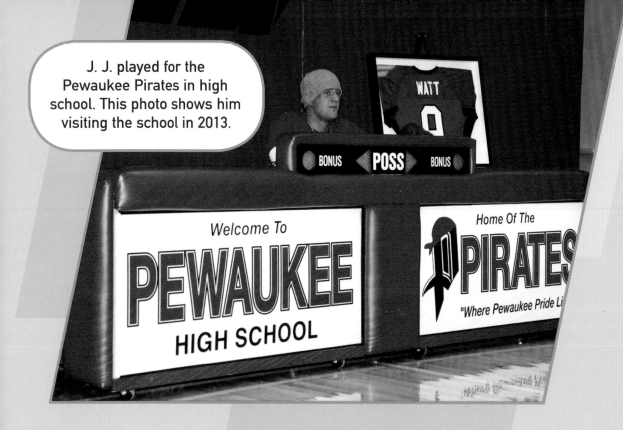

J. J. played for the Pewaukee Pirates in high school. This photo shows him visiting the school in 2013.

GROWING INTO THE GAME

J. J. was sure that he wanted to be a quarterback. He tried out for the position when the football season began at Pewaukee High School. He made the team, but not as a starting quarterback. J. J. sat on the bench for two seasons as the backup quarterback. He learned everything he could about the game and supported his team.

Playing football was only part of J. J.'s life as a high school athlete. He excelled on the basketball court and the baseball diamond. "I definitely think multiple sports are the way to go, especially in high school," J. J. said. "You only get one chance to do it."

Pewaukee hired a new football coach in 2005. Clay Iverson started J. J. at **tight end**. He also wanted the young player to try defensive end for the first time. Coach Iverson was impressed after a few games. "This kid's good, isn't he?" he said to another coach.

In 2006, J. J. took it to the next level in several sports. He averaged 13.6 points per game in basketball.

Pewaukee is about 20 minutes west of Milwaukee by car.

J. J. threw shot put in high school, like this teen.

He also tried **shot put** for the first time. J. J.'s father held the Pewaukee High School record at the time for the longest shot put. Years ago, John had hurled the metal ball 54 feet 9 inches. J. J. beat his father with a toss of 59 feet 11 inches. The huge throw set a new school record and won the Wisconsin state title. Meanwhile, J. J. had become the best player on his football team.

J. J. had worked hard to turn himself into a terrific athlete. He ate

J. J.'s shot put record didn't last long. His youngest brother, T. J., broke it a few years later. "I'm not too happy about that," J. J. joked.

In October 2012, Pewaukee High School retired J. J.'s football jersey. No one at the school will ever wear number 9 again.

healthful foods and trained to get as big and strong as possible. He stood 6 feet 5 inches tall. He weighed 235 pounds. The high school senior didn't look anything like the scrawny student he'd been a few years before.

J. J. (*left*) tackles a Purdue University player during a 2009 football game. J. J.'s team, the University of Wisconsin, won the game, 37–0.

DELIVERY GUY

J. J. was named football player of the year in his **conference** in 2006. He was also named state high school male athlete of the year by the *Milwaukee Journal Sentinel*. He was a great athlete in a variety of sports. But it was clear that his future was brightest in football.

Some of the best football colleges in the country wanted J. J. for their teams. Schools such as the University of Nebraska showed interest. He even heard from his favorite school, the University of Wisconsin. But these schools didn't offer J. J. a **scholarship**. They weren't sure he'd had enough experience in high school to play at the next level. Central Michigan University did, though. He took them up on their offer.

J. J.'s first college team, the Central Michigan Chippewas, scores a touchdown.

J. J. worked hard to become a better football player.

J. J. played 14 games as tight end for the Central Michigan Chippewas in 2007. But he wasn't happy there. J. J. left the school after one year.

College rules say that athletes must sit out for a year if they switch schools. J. J. didn't play football at all in 2008. Instead, he took classes at a **community college**. He got a job delivering pizzas for Pizza Hut to help pay for school.

In 2009, J. J. transferred to his first choice, the University of Wisconsin. He joined the team as a **walk-on**. When he wasn't working or studying, he prepared for the upcoming football season. He trained harder than ever. "It was such a good feeling to go to the gym and know that I was working my tail off to make my dream come true," J. J. said.

Before the first game of the 2009 season, Wisconsin offered J. J. a scholarship.

Seattle Seahawks star quarterback Russell Wilson also played at Wisconsin before going pro.

J. J. (*left*) was thrilled to play for Wisconsin. Here, he rushes the quarterback during a 2009 game.

The team could tell that their new player was something special. They also moved him to defensive end. J. J. played so well in 2009 that no one ever suggested he play tight end again.

He was even better in 2010. He finished second on the team in tackles and first in sacks.

J. J. bites a rose after a victory that put the University of Wisconsin on the inside track for the 2011 Rose Bowl.

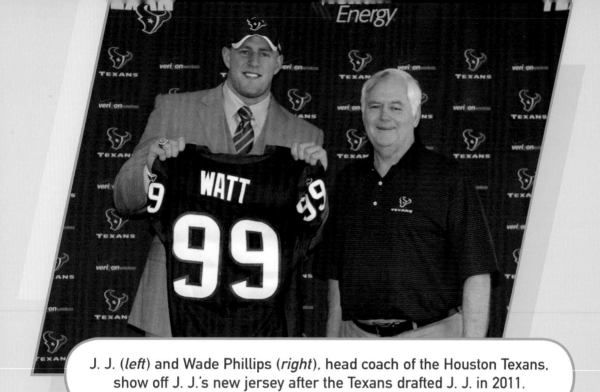

J. J. (*left*) and Wade Phillips (*right*), head coach of the Houston Texans, show off J. J.'s new jersey after the Texans drafted J. J. in 2011.

BEST SEASON EVER

J. J. had two great seasons at Wisconsin. Then he had a choice to make. Would he return to Wisconsin for one more season? Or was he ready for the NFL? He talked it over with his parents. They decided that playing in the NFL right away was a chance J. J. couldn't pass up.

"It's been a dream of mine for as long as I can remember," he said.

The Houston Texans chose J. J. with the 11th pick in the 2011 NFL **draft**. Some of the team's fans didn't like the pick. They didn't think J. J. was the most talented player available. Some Houston fans at the draft even booed when J. J.'s name was announced.

The Houston coaches had faith in J. J. He started all 16 games as a **rookie** for the Texans in 2011. He recorded 48 tackles. He also had 5.5 sacks. It

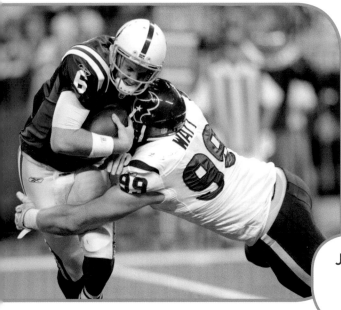

J. J. (*right*) tackles Dan Orlovsky (*left*) of the Indianapolis Colts during a 2011 NFL game.

was a good first season. But the big defensive end proved all the doubters wrong in his second year.

J. J. started 2012 on fire and didn't cool off all year. He was a sacking machine. He had at least one sack per game through Houston's first six games. By the end of the season, J. J. had racked up 20.5 sacks.

J. J. forgave the Houston fans who booed him on draft day. "This city has been nothing but great to me," he posted on Twitter.

J. J. (*left*) sacks Peyton Manning (*right*) of the Denver Broncos.

J. J. (*left*) chases down another quarterback.

He'd tied for the sixth most sacks in a season in NFL history. J. J. was great at all parts of the game in 2012. *Bleacher Report* called J. J.'s season the "most impressive in history" for a defensive lineman.

No one was surprised when J. J. was named NFL Defensive Player of the Year for 2012. He thanked his family when he received the award. "You guys taught me that if I was willing to work hard I could do anything I wanted in this world," he said.

J. J. celebrates another great game in 2012.

J. J. added 10.5 more sacks to his total in 2013. But his team still struggled. After beating the Titans in the second game of the season, the Texans didn't win again all year. Fans have faith that Houston's luck will soon change with J. J. leading the way.

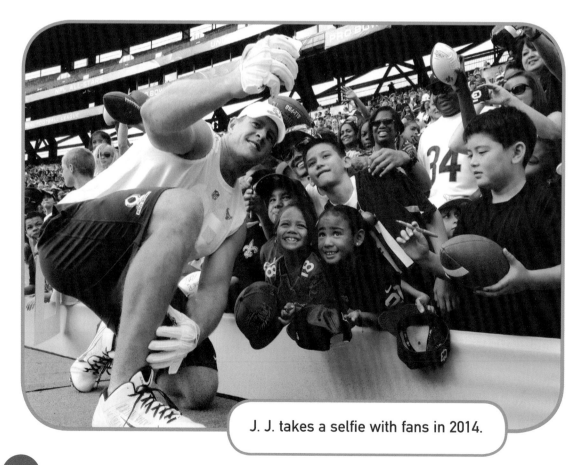

J. J. takes a selfie with fans in 2014.

Selected Career Highlights

2013   Led the Texans with 10.5 sacks

2012   Finished the season with 20.5 sacks, tied for sixth most in NFL history
Named NFL Defensive Player of the Year

2011   Started all 16 Texans games as a rookie
Drafted by the Texans

2010   Named Wisconsin team MVP
Led Wisconsin with seven sacks

2009   Played all 13 games in his first season with Wisconsin
Finished third on the team with 4.5 sacks

2008   Did not play football after switching schools

2007   Played tight end for Central Michigan University

2006   Starred on his high school team as both defensive end and tight end
Set Pewaukee High School shot put record
Named Wisconsin high school male athlete of the year by the *Milwaukee Journal Sentinel*

2005   Played defensive end for the first time

2004   Played backup quarterback for Pewaukee High School

2003   Played backup quarterback for Pewaukee High School

Glossary

community college: a college that offers courses to people living in the area and usually gives two-year degrees instead of four-year degrees

conference: a group of sports teams that play one another

defensive end: a defender who guards against the run and rushes the quarterback

draft: a yearly event in which teams take turns choosing new players from a group

offensive lineman: a player who blocks for the quarterback and the ball carriers

off-season: the part of the year when football is not played

overtime: a period of time added to the end of a game to decide a winner

punt: to kick the ball after it is dropped and before it hits the ground. A punt results in the opposing team getting control of the ball.

quarterback: a player whose main job is to throw passes

rookie: a first-year player

sack: tackling the quarterback with the football for a loss of yards

scholarship: money awarded to a student to help pay college tuition

shot put: a contest in which a heavy ball is thrown as far as possible

tight end: a player at the end of the offensive line who blocks and catches passes

tournaments: events in which teams compete to decide champions

walk-on: a player who is allowed to join a college team but is not given a scholarship

Further Reading & Websites

Fishman, Jon M. *Russell Wilson*. Minneapolis: Lerner Publications, 2015.

Kennedy, Mike, and Mark Stewart. *Touchdown: The Power and Precision of Football's Perfect Play*. Minneapolis: Millbrook Press, 2010.

NFL Website
http://www.nfl.com
The NFL's official website provides fans with recent news stories, statistics, biographies of players and coaches, and information about games.

Offical Website of the Houston Texans
http://www.houstontexans.com
The official website of the Texans includes team schedules, news, profiles of past and present players and coaches, and much more.

Sports Illustrated Kids
http://www.sikids.com
The *Sports Illustrated Kids* website covers all sports, including football.

Expand learning beyond the printed book. Download free, complementary educational resources for this book from our website, www.lernerresource.com.

Index

Photo Acknowledgments

The images in this book are used with the permission of: © George Bridges/
MCT/Getty Images, p. 4, 5; AP Photo/David J. Phillip, p. 6; AP Photo/Patric
Schneider, p. 7, 29; © Scott Halleran/Getty Images, p. 8, 9; © Louis Horch/
Dreamstime.comp. 10; © iStockphoto.com/gilaxia , p. 11; © Benis Arapovic/
Hemera/Thinkstock, p. 12; © Jamie Squire/Getty Images, p. 13; © Dwane
Lindsey, p. 15, 17; © Sandra Henderson/iStock/Thinkstock, p. 16; AP Photo/
Andy Manis, p. 18; AP Photo/Eric Canha, p. 19; AP Photo/Darron Cummings,
p. 20; AP Photo/David Stluka, p. 21; AP Photo/Morry Gash, p. 22; AP Photo/
Bill Baptist, p. 23; AP Photo/AJ Mast, p. 24; AP Photo/Jack Dempsey, p. 25; AP
Photo/Eric Gay, p. 26; AP Photo/Tony Gutierrez, p. 27; AP Photo/Oskar Garcia,
p. 28; AP Photo/Patric Schneider, p. 29.

Front Cover: © Peter G. Aiken/Getty Images

Main body text set in Caecilia LT Std 55 Roman 16/28.
Typeface provided by Adobe Systems.